MW01538017

Original title:

Cedar Whiffs Over the Mermaid Lump

Copyright © 2025 Swan Charm

Author: Sabrina Sarvik

ISBN HARDBACK: 978-1-80562-777-7

ISBN PAPERBACK: 978-1-80564-298-5

Threads of Pine and Whispering Waves

In the forest deep where the shadows play,
Whispers of pine weave tales of old,
Gentle breezes carry secrets away,
In the soft, green folds of mossy gold.

Waves of the ocean crash on the shore,
Each ripple a song of journeys untold,
Seagulls serenade, forever they soar,
While the sun dips low, turning silver to gold.

Through tangled roots where the wildflowers grow,
Butterflies dance in the dappled light,
Stories are penned in the rustle and flow,
Of nature's embrace in day and in night.

Follow the path where the shadows entwine,
Magic awakes in the heart of the glade,
Threads of the pine and the salt of the brine,
Weave a tapestry none can invade.

So linger a while where the earth meets the sky,
Let the whispers of waves guide your way,
For in every sigh, there's a reason to fly,
And in every heart, there's a dream to stay.

Echoes of Aromatic Pines

In forests thick, the whispers play,
The scent of pine, where shadows stay.
Beneath the boughs, old secrets hide,
With every breeze, the woods confide.

A carpet soft of needles green,
A world alive, yet still unseen.
The timeworn trees, they gently sway,
In twilight's glow, they softly say.

The echoes dance on wind's embrace,
An ancient hymn, a secret place.
Where tales of yore are sung anew,
A magic old, forever true.

Secrets Beneath the Tidal Veil

The ocean's breath, a misty shroud,
Hides wonders deep beneath the crowd.
Secrets whisper in the foam,
While tides in rhythm call them home.

Beneath the waves, where shadows dwell,
The coral gates, they weave a spell.
A treasure trove of dreams untold,
In depths where moonlit tales unfold.

With every crash, the waves narrate,
The stories of the sea's own fate.
Adventures spin in salty air,
As mermaids pause, their hearts laid bare.

Fantasies in Driftwood Shadows

Upon the shore, where driftwoods lie,
The fantasies of night draw nigh.
Each twisted form a tale enfold,
Of sailors' dreams and legends bold.

In twilight's grasp, the shadows blend,
The whispers twine, their voices send.
From polished grains, stories arise,
As starlit waves compose the skies.

The breeze caresses each old frame,
With every touch, it calls their name.
As night unfolds, the visions soar,
A dance of dreams upon the shore.

Whispering Conifers Unite

Beneath the canopy where shadows fall,
The conifers whisper, a tale for all.
With needles green, they weave their song,
In harmony, they hum along.

The winds join in, a symphonic swell,
In twilight's glow, a magic spell.
Each trunk a vessel of stories deep,
While dusk settles, the forest keeps.

The gentle sway, the rustling sound,
In every note, enchantments found.
Together they stand, a timeless choir,
In nature's breath, they never tire.

The Confluence of Aroma and Sea

The salty breeze sweeps through the air,
With hints of jasmine, a fragrant flare.
Waves whisper secrets as they collide,
While oceans dance with sweetness wide.

Sunsets breathe hues of golden glow,
Where tides of lavender ebb and flow.
Each scent a story, ancient and deep,
In the realm where dreams and waters seep.

The confluence blooms, a wild embrace,
Nature's perfume, a soft, warm trace.
Beneath the stars that twinkle and gleam,
The world enchants, like a waking dream.

Fables on the Edge of the Shore

Upon the rocks where legends rest,
Whispers of fables cling to the crest.
The ocean hums an ancient tune,
As gulls weave tales beneath the moon.

Shells hold secrets from times gone by,
Each grain of sand a tale awry.
Footprints washed away in the tide,
Echoes of stories that swell with pride.

Fables unfold with the rising sun,
As waves roll in and shadows run.
Timeless whispers in the briny air,
Where myth and reality blend with care.

Hidden Currents of Lush Delight

In the heart of the cove, where the wildflowers grow,
Hidden currents twist, ebbing soft and low.
Whispers of verde, scents rich and sweet,
Invite the wanderer to rest their feet.

Mossy banks cradle the flow of the stream,
Reflecting the light, like a glimmering dream.
Petals unfold, flushed with morning dew,
A dance of colors, pure and true.

Each ripple holds joy, each rustle a cheer,
Nature's own symphony sung clear.
In this secret place where wonders dwell,
A tale of delight, one can't help but tell.

Murmurs of the Wind and Tide

Murmurs rise softly from deep, rolling foam,
Echoing softly, they guide us home.
A serenade sung by the stars above,
Where whispers of love blend with the dove.

Breezes caress like a lover's hand,
As the tide flutters across the sand.
Crickets respond with a gentle plea,
In the language of dusk, both wild and free.

The night wraps around like a warm embrace,
Bathing the shore in a silvery lace.
Murmurs of the wind mix with the tide,
Crafting a melody nature won't hide.

Harmony of Pine and Ocean Depths

In the whispering pines, where the sea meets the shore,
The laughter of waves brings a soft, soothing score.
Moss blankets the ground, a cushion so rare,
While breezes entwine with the salt in the air.

Above, gulls are dancing in the cobalt sky,
Nature's sweet symphony, a gentle goodbye.
Where ocean and forest in beauty align,
A tapestry woven in colors divine.

Sylvan soft echoes, the lapping tides speak,
As secrets of ages unveil from the creek.
Oh, harmony singing, a timeless embrace,
Nature's own song, in this magical place.

The Allure of Tidal Aromas

The tide rolls in with a silken caress,
Bringing scents of the ocean, a fragrant dress.
Seaweed and salt dance on the warm, gentle breeze,
While sun blinks playfully through rustling trees.

Each wave bears whispers of stories untold,
Of ships lost and found, of treasures and gold.
The drum of the ocean, the rhythm of time,
In harmony mingling, a perfect rhyme.

With each passing tide, mystery unfurls,
In the heart of the sea, as the seagull twirls.
A potion of wonders, with scents to enthrall,
The allurement of tides, a call to us all.

Celestial Waters and Forest Murmurs

Moonbeams cascade on a shimmering tide,
Where celestial waters in silence reside.
The forest extends with its secrets so deep,
As stars wink above, while the world lies asleep.

Glistening droplets on leaves shimmer bright,
Whispers of magic in the cool, velvet night.
With every soft murmur, the night comes alive,
In the velvet embrace, the dreams start to thrive.

Reflections of starlight, the sky's gentle kiss,
Invite us to wander, to linger in bliss.
Through shadows and glimmers, a world still unknown,
Celestial dance, where the heart feels at home.

Enchanted Roots by the Water's Edge

Rooted in whispers, the ancient trees stand,
Guardians of secrets in this timeless land.
By the water's edge, where the soft currents flow,
An enchanted realm where the wildflowers grow.

Trickling streams sing a lullaby sweet,
To the rhythm of nature beneath our bare feet.
Glimmers of sunlight weave through the green,
A tapestry shaded, serene and unseen.

In the embrace of the roots, life breathes anew,
Each twist tells a story, a legend or two.
The magic erupts where land kisses sea,
Enchantment awaits in this sanctuary free.

Aromas from Ancient Forests

In shadows deep where whispers dwell,
The ancient boughs weave tales to tell.
With every breath, the mossy ground,
Holds secrets lost, yet still profound.

The fragrant pine, the cedar's sigh,
Embrace the breeze that wanders by.
Through tangled roots, the spirits play,
In nature's arms, they yearn to stay.

Soft sunlight drapes in golden streams,
While dappled leaves join in my dreams.
The air, a blend of earth and rain,
Calls forth the past, a sweet refrain.

Salty Air Meets Wooded Grace

Upon the shore where land meets sea,
The salty air sings songs to me.
With whispers soft from forest green,
A harmony unseen, serene.

The ocean's breath, a wild embrace,
Mingles with trees in gentle grace.
As waves applaud the rugged coast,
In unity, they blend the most.

The seagulls cry, a joyful sound,
While wooden trails stretch all around.
In twilight's glow, my heart takes flight,
Where sea and forest merge in light.

Embracing the Tide's Perfume

The tide rolls in with fragrant waves,
Each crest a tale that nature braves.
With seaweed's scent and briny kiss,
I find a world of tranquil bliss.

Upon the rocks where barnacles cling,
The whispers of the ocean sing.
A dance of shells, as sunbeams sprawl,
In harmony, they heed the call.

The foam, a lace of white delight,
Embraces shore and paints the night.
Here in the dusk, my spirit roams,
In every wave, I find my home.

Tales Woven in Ocean Spray

In swirling mist where legends hide,
The ocean's breath is wild and wide.
With every splash, a story swells,
Of ships and souls, of whispered spells.

The salty spray, a poet's muse,
It captures dreams we cannot lose.
From sandy shores to distant lands,
Adventure calls with open hands.

Oh, how the waves embrace the shore,
A rhythmic dance forevermore.
In ocean spray, our hearts ignite,
As tales unfold in starry night.

Glistening Shores and Evergreen Whispers

Where sunlight dances on the tide,
The waves unfold their soft embrace.
Among the pines, where dreams reside,
The whispers carry time and space.

Golden sands stretch far and wide,
As echoes of the sea-foam play.
With every step, the heart's a guide,
To hidden realms where shadows sway.

Beneath the sky, so crisp and blue,
The gulls in spirals gently glide.
In twilight's glow, the world feels new,
And secrets breathe where hearts confide.

With every ripple, stories wake,
In salty air, sweet memories soar.
The shores, they cradle every ache,
As moonlight paints the ocean's floor.

Evergreen whispers call the night,
Entwined with laughter, magic's grace.
In every heart lies pure delight,
On glistening shores, our souls embrace.

Sirens' Secrets in the Cedar Shade

In quiet groves where shadows loom,
Beneath the cedar's ancient boughs.
The sirens sing of lost perfume,
Enchanting hearts with whispered vows.

Their voices ripple through the air,
Like silver threads that weave a tale.
They beckon those who dare to dare,
And wander 'neath the twilight veil.

The twilight dances with the moon,
As creatures of the night awake.
In secret dreams, they hum a tune,
Inviting souls, their hearts to stake.

A hidden path, a shimmering light,
Leads seekers to the fabled glen.
In cedar shade, all feels so right,
Where magic brews again, again.

While stars above weave silver seams,
The sirens take the world aglow.
With every heart revealed in dreams,
Their secrets linger, soft and slow.

Driftwood Chronicles of the Green Isle

Upon the shores of stories old,
Where driftwood whispers tales untold.
The sea brings treasures from afar,
Each piece a memory, a star.

The winds entwine with salt and sand,
As currents shape the sculptor's hand.
With every wave, a journey starts,
Of lonely souls and yearning hearts.

In craggy coves, the echoes blend,
Of laughter shared, of lovers lost.
The driftwood knows, it has no end,
Yet carries love, despite the cost.

The tides will shift, the world will change,
But in these woods, there's warmth, it's strange.
Each story sewn into the bark,
Of whispered dreams igniting spark.

As night descends, the stars awake,
With ancient wisdom, they will lend.
The chronicles will never break,
For on this isle, all paths transcend.

Salty Air and Woodland Mystique

In tangled woods where shadows play,
The salty air brings tales anew.
With every turn, the heart may sway,
As magic lingers in the dew.

Beneath the boughs, the whispers swish,
Of creatures hiding in the glade.
The moonlit path, a timeless wish,
Awakens all the dreams we've made.

With every breeze, a secret shared,
In woodland depths, enchantment swells.
The nature round, forever bared,
Unfolds the stories that it tells.

The ceaseless ebb of waves nearby,
Reminds us of the tides of fate.
In salty air, we learn to fly,
As if our souls can re-create.

So linger here, beneath the trees,
Where woodland mystique wraps its arms.
Within the heart, the spirit sees,
The world enchant with all its charms.

Brushstrokes with Liquid Breezes

In twilight's glow, the colors sway,
A canvas kissed by end of day.
With liquid brushes, dreams unfurl,
Painting whispers, a secret world.

Azure skies and gold leaf streams,
Crafting all a heart can dream.
Through swirls of night and shades of sound,
A symphony of hues abound.

The breezes dance, a painter's hand,
In every stroke, the sea, the sand.
As silence falls, the colors gleam,
In hues of hope, we dare to dream.

With each soft brush, a story told,
Of warmth, of love, of shimmered gold.
The brushstrokes weave, a magic draw,
In every heart, inspiring awe.

A blurred horizon, a fading light,
In every stroke, a star ignites.
The world, a canvas, vast and wide,
Each liquid breeze, a joyful ride.

Haikus Beneath the Tides

Beneath the calm waves,
Secrets of the ocean rest,
Silent whispers breathe.

Shimmering moonlight,
Guides the tide's gentle embrace,
Dreams in liquid night.

Echoes of the deep,
In every wave, a heartbeat,
Nature's lullaby.

Coral gardens bloom,
Fragrant colors softly sway,
Life's dance in the tide.

Stars above us shine,
While below, a world unknown,
Nature's harmony.

In the Company of Mermaids and Pines

In shadowed groves, the story flows,
With mermaids' songs and pine trees' prose.
Their laughter weaves through branches tall,
A playful breeze, enchanting call.

Beneath the surface, magic glows,
In whispers shared where the river flows.
Mermaids dance, with shimmering tails,
As the forest hums soft, soothing tales.

Fingers of light through needles stretch,
An ancient bond that none may fetch.
With seashell dreams and forest sighs,
Together they dwell, beneath the skies.

Round twilight's edge, secrets entwine,
With every breeze, our hearts align.
In harmony, as stars alight,
We find our magic in the night.

The touch of waves wraps round like thread,
While pines above guard all that's said.
In company found, both fierce and kind,
A spirit of nature, heart entwined.

Songs of the Surface and Below

From deep within, the ocean sings,
A chorus bright as each wave springs.
Above, the dance of sunlight plays,
While shadows weave in cool, soft bays.

The clash of tides in rhythmic flow,
A melody of ebb and glow.
Each creature hums a living note,
Together in a song, they float.

Above the waves, the world takes flight,
Birds mirror the dusk, soft and light.
With every beat from wave to shore,
A harmony we can't ignore.

Beneath the surface, secrets dwell,
In silent depths where whispers swell.
An underwater symphony,
Sings of life in perfect harmony.

Together, they weave a timeless thread,
Of songs we hear and tales unsaid.
In the dance of water's embrace,
We find our truths, our sacred space.

Serene Shores and Whispering Trees

Beneath the sky so wide and blue,
The gentle waves do softly sing,
With whispers carried on the breeze,
And secrets wrapped in emerald green.

The sand, like sugar, cool and fine,
Awaits the dance of fleeting feet,
While branches sway in graceful lines,
Their leaves perform a soft retreat.

The sun dips low, a golden hue,
As moonlight bathes the world aglow,
And dreams take flight in twilight air,
Where tides of hope and wishes flow.

With twilight's brush, the stars appear,
Each twinkle holds a tale untold,
The melodies of night we hear,
In harmony with silence bold.

In whispers soft and spirits free,
The shores and trees in union stand,
A quiet peace—a remedy,
For wanderers in this enchanted land.

Vagabond Songs of Salt and Earth

Upon the wind, a song takes flight,
Of sandy shores and distant lands,
Where sailors' dreams meet the moon's light,
And tides weave tales with caring hands.

The salt-stung breezes call my name,
A symphony of lost desires,
With every wave, a whispered claim,
From depths where ancient spirit fires.

The earth beneath my wandering feet,
Cradles secrets of long ago,
In every step, a heartbeat sweet,
The call of life—a vibrant glow.

Across the hills, through valleys deep,
My heart, a compass, leads the way,
To sunlit shores where shadows sleep,
With every dawn, a bright ballet.

The ocean's song and whispered earth,
Together form a tapestry,
A life of wonder, joy, and mirth,
For every dreamer's heart to see.

Twilight Tales of the Ocean's Edge

When twilight steals the day away,
And golden rays begin to fade,
The ocean whispers tales of play,
In hidden depths, the dreams are laid.

The waves, like soft caresses flow,
With stories woven in their might,
Of sailors brave and hearts aglow,
Adventures born beneath the night.

A silver moon begins to rise,
Reflecting hopes upon the sea,
In every crest, a thousand sighs,
The echoes sing of what will be.

With salty air and stars in view,
The ocean's edge invites the bold,
Where shadows dance and wishes strew,
A treasure chest of stories told.

So gather near, ye dreamers dear,
Let twilight's magic hold you tight,
For in this realm of peace and cheer,
The ocean sings through endless night.

Echoing Whispers of the Treetop Mermaids

High above where branches weave,
In emerald canopies they dwell,
The mermaids of the forest leave,
Their echoes in a secret spell.

With laughter gentle as the breeze,
They sing to all the wandering souls,
In quiet pools beneath the trees,
Where nature keeps its sacred scrolls.

Each rustling leaf tells stories bold,
Of ancient mysteries held in trust,
While sunlight dapples, bright and gold,
The whispers weave through verdant dust.

In twilight hours, when shadows play,
The mermaids twirl in moonlit glee,
Their magic wraps the night in sway,
And nature dances wild and free.

So heed the call of woodland grace,
For every echo holds a dream,
In every corner, a smiling face,
Where treetop mermaids softly beam.

Nature's Secret Symphony

In shadows deep where whispers play,
The leaves entwine in soft ballet.
A rustle speaks, a song unfolds,
As nature's heart in silence holds.

The brook hums low, a gentle tune,
Beneath the watchful, silver moon.
Each rippling note, a tale of old,
In water's dance, the world unfolds.

The wind weaves paths through branches wide,
With every breeze, a secret guide.
It carries tales from dusk till dawn,
In nature's arms, we're never drawn.

A symphony of light and shade,
In hidden groves where dreams are laid.
The beauty rests in quiet grace,
In nature's love, we find our place.

Enchanted Roots Beneath the Surface

Beneath the ground, in earth so still,
The roots entwine with unseen will.
They stretch and weave, a vibrant thread,
In whispered tales of life, long dead.

Through tangled paths and shadows deep,
The secrets of the forest keep.
With every twist, a story spun,
Of battles fought and races run.

The roots will sigh as seasons change,
In rhythms rich and life so strange.
Their silent strength, a bond so tight,
In darkness where they gain their light.

And every flower that blooms above,
Whispers tales of strength and love.
In hidden worlds where wonders lie,
The roots connect and never die.

The Canvas of Scented Currents

Upon the breeze, a fragrance drifts,
Of blooming flowers, nature's gifts.
The canvas sways with colors bright,
As scents emerge in morning light.

With every gust, a story spins,
Of summer's joys and winter's sins.
The air is thick with whispered charms,
A dance of blooms, forgotten farms.

The honeysuckle, sweet and bold,
Reveals the tales that time has told.
While lavender weaves dreams so fair,
In scented currents, we find air.

Each moment drapes a pastel hue,
Of nature's paint, the old, the new.
The magic flows where spirits soar,
In every waft, we'll seek for more.

Breaths of Salt and Evergreen

In ocean's kiss, the salt does sing,
With breezes fresh, the wild winds bring.
A dance of waves in rhythmic grace,
Where sea and sky embrace their space.

Among the pines, the whispers rise,
As secrets float to azure skies.
Each needle sharp, a tale of time,
In breaths of green, a life sublime.

The waves will wash the shores away,
Yet evermore they'll find their way.
Each crest and trough, an endless quest,
In nature's arms, we find our rest.

The salt and spruce blend soft and sweet,
A symphony where earth and sea meet.
In every breath, a world begun,
In salted air, our hearts are one.

Beneath the Waves

In the depth where silence sings,
Mermaids weave their secret rings.
Coral castles, bright and bold,
Guard the stories yet untold.

Fish like rainbows dance and play,
In the twilight, soft and gray.
Echoes of the ocean's might,
Whispers fade into the night.

Seahorses drift with grace and poise,
Singing sweetly, ocean's voice.
Gentle currents carry dreams,
Flowing softly, moonlight gleams.

Pearls of wisdom found in shells,
Guarding secrets, ancient spells.
As tides rise and fall anew,
Waves will always carry you.

Among the Trees

In emerald groves where stories dwell,
Whispers echo, weaving spells.
Branches stretch like arms in flight,
Cradling dreams in soft moonlight.

Beneath the boughs, the shadows play,
Frogs croak softly, night meets day.
Owls watch with their knowing eyes,
Guardians beneath the starlit skies.

Leaves flutter down like whispered lore,
Carried on the breeze to explore.
With every rustle, quite profound,
Nature's secrets can be found.

Among the roots where wisdom grows,
Every heartbeat, life bestows.
A tapestry of green and gold,
Woven tales that must be told.

Mysteries of the Nautical Forest

Where water meets the wood so deep,
Mysteries in shadow creep.
Fish and fowl in harmony,
Dance beneath a canopy.

Rippling streams like ribbons flow,
Guiding secrets only they know.
Sunlight filters, golden sheen,
Life unfolds in spaces between.

Among the roots, the otters glide,
In the current, they take pride.
Every ripple tells a tale,
Of adventures beyond the pale.

Fern and kelp in a sweet embrace,
Form a world, a sacred space.
Where earth and ocean's spirits twine,
In this realm, all hearts align.

Scented Tides and Aquatic Tales

Scented tides on the evening breeze,
Carry whispers of ancient seas.
From surf to shore, the stories rise,
Unfolding 'neath the starry skies.

Seashells gather like treasures rare,
Holding secrets beyond compare.
Waves embrace the sandy strand,
Weaving dreams on the golden sand.

The ocean's song, a lullaby,
Cradling heartbeats, soft and shy.
With every crash, the tide reveals,
The beauty that the sea conceals.

Dolphins leap, a joyous sight,
Painting ripples in the night.
In this dance of water and light,
Life awakens, pure delight.

Lullabies of the Beach and Boughs

The beach sings soft, like a gentle hand,
Caressing dreams upon the sand.
Each wave a whisper, smooth and low,
Carving stories as they flow.

Tall trees sway in the cooling breeze,
Rustling leaves like ancient pleas.
Together in harmony they roam,
Creating magic, calling home.

Moonlit paths on the water's face,
Infused with peace, a sacred space.
Footprints left on twilight's shore,
Tell of journeys, legends bore.

In lullabies, the world unwinds,
Where ocean dreams and forest finds.
With every breath, the soul takes flight,
In this realm of pure delight.

Fisherman's Folklore

In twilight's glow, the boats set sail,
Old tales rise up with every gale.
Whispers of fish in the ocean's dance,
Echo the dreams of a seafarer's chance.

The nets cast wide, the waves do sigh,
Under the watch of a shadowed sky.
Each kraken's tale, a sailor's jest,
In a world where the brave are truly blessed.

The barnacles cling to the rocky shore,
Tales of lost treasures and adventures galore.
Every ripple holds a secret deep,
A fisherman's heart in the ocean's keep.

With every catch, there's a story spun,
Of moonlit nights and the rising sun.
The sea, a canvas where legends thrive,
In each wave's song, the past comes alive.

So raise a toast to the tides that bind,
To the salty air that soothes the mind.
For in a fisherman's heart, you'll see,
The timeless bond between ocean and sea.

Aromatic Pines

In woods where whispers softly wane,
The aroma of pines, a sweet refrain.
Sunlight dapples through the green,
Nature's breath, pure and serene.

Moss blankets paths where children roam,
Beneath the canopy, they find their home.
Each rustle tells of creatures near,
In this embrace, nothing is unclear.

The gentle breeze through needles weaves,
Secrets linger among rustling leaves.
A symphony played by nature's hand,
Invoking dreams in this enchanted land.

Starlit nights with a whispered tune,
While fireflies dance beneath the moon.
The scent of pine, a lover's sigh,
In fragrant woods where spirits fly.

So stroll these paths where memories twine,
Where heart and nature, forever align.
In every breath, find peace and grace,
In aromatic pines, our sacred space.

The Lure of Brine and Boughs

Where the brine meets the forest's call,
Whispers of wonder reach high and small.
A tale of tides and trees entwined,
The lure of both is perfectly aligned.

Seagulls cry above the crashing wave,
While ancient boughs stand proud and brave.
Each breeze that blows tells stories old,
Of sailors bold and waters cold.

Twilight shines on the foam-kissed shore,
While leafy canopies hold tales of yore.
The rhythm of brine, the rustle of leaves,
In this world, the heart believes.

Oceans tumbling over sandy gifts,
Boughs embracing every shift.
Nature's song plays soft and bright,
In the fusion of day and night.

So linger here where both worlds meet,
Let brine and boughs weave a bittersweet.
In every sound, sailors' dreams abide,
In the dance of the tides, side by side.

Fables of the Sea and Sylvan Air

Listen close to the fables spun,
Of depths unknown and forests run.
Where the ocean kisses roots so deep,
And secrets of both awaken from sleep.

The sea's embrace, both wild and free,
Ignores the bounds of land and tree.
Each legend carved by time's own hand,
Speaks of the magic in sea and land.

Gentle whispers of waves on shore,
Mingle with calls of the forest floor.
In every echo, a tale is born,
Of sailors lost and a new day's dawn.

Through misty sighs where the sea meets wood,
Lies the heart of adventure, misunderstood.
A hearth of dreams, a place of lore,
Where fables breathe forevermore.

So take a step through twilight's haze,
Embrace the magic of the waves.
For in the tapestry of sky and sea,
Lies the endless quest for you and me.

Midnight Mist and Marine Melodies

In midnight mist, the ocean hums,
A lullaby to the sailor who comes.
Waves crash gently, a soothing sound,
In the cloak of darkness, peace is found.

Stars twinkle bright in the velvet night,
Each glimmer a promise, a hopeful light.
As tides ebb, they sway and flow,
Carrying dreams where the wild winds blow.

Whispers of salt in the cool embrace,
Drift through the air like a lover's grace.
With every note of the marine's song,
Echoes of friendship, where all belong.

The mist wraps tight in a soft cocoon,
As the ocean dances beneath the moon.
Each melody sings of love and loss,
In the stillness, we find what's embossed.

So sail on waves that cradle the soul,
Let marine melodies make you whole.
For in the heart of midnight's spell,
Lies a world where every dream can dwell.

Letters from the Algae's Embrace

In silence deep where tides do sigh,
Algae whispers, secrets nigh,
Carried forth by currents bold,
Stories ancient, yet untold.

With tendrils green and fingers wet,
Nature's ink, within the jet,
You'll find the echoes of the sea,
A letter penned in harmony.

Beneath the surface, colors swirl,
Threads of gold in water curl,
From myriad depths, the voices blend,
An ode to life that shall not end.

Twinkling stars on waves do rest,
In algae's arms, one feels the blessed,
Each bloom a tale, a breath of light,
Crafting dreams from day to night.

So heed the hush, the ocean's call,
From algae's heart, we've heard it all,
In every splash, in every stream,
A watery dance, a whispering dream.

An Odyssey of Aroma and Tide

Upon the shore where breezes play,
Scented memories come to sway,
Salt and sea entwine like lace,
An odyssey through time and space.

Waves bring whispers of distant lands,
Carried forth by unseen hands,
Aromas wild, both sweet and bold,
Stories of sailors, brave and old.

Citrus bursts mix with briny zest,
Each note a journey, a loving quest,
Whirling fragrances dance and glide,
An embrace of ocean and tide.

With every tide, a shift renews,
A melody of varied hues,
From clover sweet to distant pine,
The essence of the divine.

So let us wander, hearts aflame,
Through aromatic paths we claim,
In every wave, a tale awaits,
An odyssey that resonates.

Elysium Under the Whispering Pines

In a vale where shadows play,
Whispering pines at close of day,
Dreams cascade in emerald light,
Elysium found in tranquil night.

Moonbeams weave through branches tall,
A symphony of nature's call,
With every breath, the forest sighs,
A secret world beneath the skies.

Gentle creatures prance and glide,
Where magic brews and spirits bide,
In every rustle, tales unfold,
Of ancient spirits, brave and bold.

Grasses sway in rhythms sweet,
A dance of life, where heartbeats meet,
In this haven, time stands still,
Under pines, our dreams fulfill.

So linger here where wishes bloom,
In nature's heart, dispelling gloom,
Embrace the night, let day depart,
Elysium rests within the heart.

The Dance of Rot and Sea Glass

Upon the shore, where time decays,
The dance of rot begins to play,
With sea glass shards, and driftwood's grace,
A tapestry of time and space.

In the mingling of the old and new,
The ocean spins a tale so true,
Colors clash in vibrant display,
A ballet forged from night and day.

From crumbling shells to coral's plea,
Nature's art speaks, wild and free,
Amidst the chaos, beauty glows,
In every wave, a story flows.

Soft whispers carried on the breeze,
Memories drift with careless ease,
With each new tide, fresh tales are spun,
A dance of life, forever won.

So take a moment, breathe it in,
The dance of rot, where all begins,
With sea glass bright, and memories cast,
A reminder that nothing lasts.

Scented Breezes and Ocean Dreams

On the breeze, the flowers dance,
Carried far in a wistful glance.
Whispers of salt and thyme entwine,
In the twilight where hearts align.

Golden sun meets the silver sea,
As whispers echo, wild and free.
Footprints fade on the sandy shore,
Tales of the mermaid's ocean lore.

Shells that sing from depths untold,
Secrets of waves and legends old.
A fragrance sweet, a promise clear,
In every breeze, the heart can hear.

Dreams take flight on the evening tide,
Where starry secrets gently bide.
In the lull between dusk and dawn,
The sea's embrace, forever drawn.

Waves that laugh and whisper true,
In their magic, we find our due.
With scented breezes, hopes will gleam,
Forever lost in ocean dreams.

The Mermaid's Fragrant Lure

Beneath the waves where shadows play,
Lies a world of wonder, bright as day.
A fragrant song that beckons near,
From silken strands and voices clear.

The moonlit tide reveals her grace,
A shimmering tail, a flawless trace.
In the depths, her laughter glows,
Where the secrets of the ocean flow.

Jasmine blooms in the salty air,
With every note, a whispered prayer.
The ocean's call, an endless tune,
Echoes softly beneath the moon.

Shells aglow with a golden blush,
Where the heart feels a gentle hush.
The mermaid's lure, a tender art,
A tapestry woven within the heart.

With tides that rise and gently swell,
In her embrace, all dreams do dwell.
A fragrant breeze, a dazzling swirl,
In the depths of night, the mermaid's pearl.

Lullabies of Forest and Sea

In the heart of the woods, where shadows weave,
Nature sings, and spirits believe.
A lullaby soft through branches flows,
With notes of love the evening knows.

Moonbeams dance on the ocean's crest,
Calling forth dreams, inviting rest.
The forest hums with a soothing sigh,
As starlit whispers drift on by.

In the twilight, a fawn draws near,
While the waves murmur, sweet and clear.
This gentle blend of earth and tide,
In lullabies, the worlds collide.

With every crickets' hidden song,
Nature's chorus echoes strong.
Forest and sea, in harmony,
Cradle the night in unity.

The tides pull back, the trees lean low,
In secret dreams, the spirits grow.
With lullabies of love so free,
In every heart, the earth and sea.

Enchanted Mists at Waters' Edge

In the dawn, where mists arise,
Veils of magic cloak the skies.
With gentle strokes, the water's edge,
Holds secrets swathed in twilight's pledge.

Softly woven through the trees,
Echoes of laughter in the breeze.
Each drop of dew, a wishful dream,
Wrapped in the river's silver gleam.

Footprints vanish, shadows blend,
As spirits of the water wend.
Whispers float through the morning light,
Chasing the remnants of the night.

When silver clouds and waters kiss,
In the hush, we find our bliss.
Enchanted mists that softly tread,
Awake the magic where we're led.

Beneath the surface, stories lie,
Of forgotten realms and reason why.
At waters' edge, with hearts we wage,
A dance of dreams in mists engage.

The Poetry of Tides and Timber

The whispering winds call the trees,
Their branches sway with gentle ease.
As waves crash down on sandy shore,
Nature's song forevermore.

The tide pulls back with magic grace,
Leaving footprints, a fleeting trace.
Timber stands tall, wise and old,
Together they weave stories told.

From salt-kissed breeze to mossy glades,
In harmony, the world cascades.
Each tide that ebbs and flows anew,
Brings secrets that the sea once knew.

Through twilight's glow, the colors bloom,
In forest deep, where shadows loom.
The dance of light on water's skin,
A place where dreams and life begin.

Listen close, the world will speak,
In every wave, a tale unique.
The poetry of tides and trees,
Brings heart and soul eternal peace.

A Journey Through Timbered Whispers

In the forest, shadows play,
Whispers of the wood on display.
Each step a note in nature's song,
Echoes guiding us along.

Timbered giants, standing proud,
Guard secrets lost in a shroud.
Beneath their canopies we roam,
Finding in the wild our home.

A breeze carries the scent of pine,
Blending earth with the divine.
Each rustle speaks of tales untold,
A journey where our hearts unfold.

Moonlight dances through the leaves,
Casting spells that nature weaves.
In timbered whispers, we explore,
The magic lies forevermore.

With every rustle, a spark ignites,
In the depths of enchanting nights.
Through timbered paths, our spirits soar,
United with the earth's deep core.

Ocean Reverie and Woody Hues

In salty air, the dreams take flight,
Ocean waves calling through the night.
Whispers of brine combine with wood,
Nature's palette, free and good.

The foam caresses the rugged stone,
While forests hum in a soft tone.
Each color blends, a vibrant hue,
A dance of nature, fresh and new.

Beneath the waves, life's secrets hide,
In driftwood tales where tides reside.
The ocean's heart, a treasure trove,
Through wooded shores, our spirits rove.

In dreamy nights, the stories swell,
Of maritime lore we long to tell.
In harmony, the sea and tree,
Grant sweet reveries wild and free.

The taste of salt, the scent of pine,
Together weave a life divine.
In ocean's merry, woody hues,
Our souls find solace, hearts renew.

The Lure of Scent and Wave

A siren's call on the ocean's breath,
Where scent of salt meets earthy depth.
The pine trees sway, a welcoming sight,
In the dance of day and the embrace of night.

Waves build stories on the shore,
Each crest a promise, each crash implores.
A whisper of jasmine, a hint of breeze,
Nature's perfume carried with ease.

The timber sings in harmony's key,
A melody soft, wild, and free.
In the rustle of leaves, the waves agree,
Life's perfume blossoms eternally.

With each moment, a fragrant tale,
Salt and cedar on the wind set sail.
Hands of nature craft this blend,
A lure of scent, where dreams transcend.

So, let us wander, hearts in tow,
To places where rivers and oceans flow.
In scent and wave, our spirits roam,
Nature's lullaby, forever home.

Seaside Echoes of Enchanted Pines

In the twilight glow, where the shadows dance,
Whispers of magic in a wistful chance.
The pines stand tall, with stories to share,
Echoes of dreams linger in the air.

Waves crash softly, a lullaby sweet,
As the tide retreats, hearts skip a beat.
With shells scattered wide, treasures unfold,
Secrets of the ocean, in whispers retold.

Beneath the stars, where the wild things roam,
Fables of mermaids lead sailors back home.
The scent of salt mingles with pine,
Timeless enchantment, forever divine.

Footprints in sand, tales left behind,
Memories woven, intricately entwined.
In the shimmering light, the past comes alive,
As echoes of laughter in the surf still thrive.

So let's wander together, hand in hand,
Through enchanted forests, on golden sand.
With every heartbeat, magic's our guide,
In seaside echoes where dreams still abide.

Oceanic Dreams Beneath the Dunes

Under the moon's gaze, the dunes gleam bright,
Whispers of oceans call through the night.
In silken sand, our footprints align,
Sketching our stories, we're two hearts entwined.

Stars overhead twinkle like tiny gems,
Each wave that crashes, a new poem stems.
Seashells await, with secrets to tell,
In the hush of the night, they cast their spell.

Mirrors of water reflect the deep sky,
Where dreams take flight and the spirits fly.
With each gentle breeze, the night holds its breath,
In the arms of the ocean, we dance with death.

Wandering pathways of silver and gold,
We chase the horizon, where stories unfold.
In the embrace of the seas, we find our tune,
The world fades away, under the watchful moon.

With laughter and love, we weave through the sand,
Each moment, a treasure, perfectly planned.
Together we dream, our souls in a trance,
Beneath the dunes, in a mystical dance.

Aromas of the Siren's Grove

In the heart of the grove, where shadows meet light,
Aromas of sea breeze, in whispers take flight.
Each petal and leaf carries tales of the deep,
Secrets of sirens in slumbering sleep.

The fragrance of jasmine mingles with brine,
Enchanting the senses, a melody fine.
Where echoes of laughter twirl in the air,
The grove holds its magic, beyond compare.

Drifting on breezes, the scents intertwine,
With each fragrant breath, our souls start to shine.
In twilight's embrace, the world fades away,
As siren songs beckon, urging us to stay.

The shimmering leaves dance, a silvery waltz,
In harmony, nature remembers its pulse.
We stand in the glow, enchanted and free,
Surrounded by whispers of what's yet to be.

So here in the grove, where the wild things grow,
We'll remain forever, hearts wrapped in glow.
With the sirens as guardians, our spirits take flight,
In the aromas of magic, we find pure delight.

The Whispering Breeze of Ocean's Song

In the dawn's embrace, where the sea meets the sky,
The breeze whispers softly, like a lover's sigh.
With each gentle touch, it calls out our name,
An invitation sweet, to dance in its frame.

Waves roll in rhythm, a symphony grand,
As we twirl with the tides, hand in hand.
The ocean's song flows, a lullaby clear,
In its tender embrace, all worries disappear.

With laughter like bubbles, we skip on the shore,
Each footstep a treasure, a wish to explore.
Carried by currents, our dreams take flight,
Under sails of the sunset, painted in light.

As moonlight bathes all in a silvery glow,
The whispering breeze shares tales of the flow.
In the night's gentle arms, stars start to sing,
With hearts wide open, we're free as the wing.

So let us remember, through shadows unmet,
The magic of moments we'll never forget.
In the whispering breeze, our spirits are strong,
Forever entwined in the ocean's sweet song.

Whims of the Pilot Whale's Song

In twilight's hush, a tune did rise,
A symphony beneath the skies.
Deep waters churned, a velvet sway,
Echoes danced as daylight gave way.

With every note the heart entwined,
A tale of currents, soft and kind.
Whale calls twinkled through the blue,
A serenade for me and you.

They sang of joy, they sang of woe,
Of depths concealed where secrets grow.
In harmony, their voices blend,
A timeless song that will not end.

Around the boat, the whispers stirred,
In tides of dreams, the music blurred.
Each gasp for air a fleeting spark,
Their hidden world, a deep, vast arc.

As night unfurls its starry shroud,
The pilot whales sing, proud and loud.
A journey through the ocean wide,
In melody and waves, we glide.

Moon-touched Waters and Leafy Sentinels

Beneath the moon, the waters gleam,
A silver path, a whispered dream.
The leaves above like watchful eyes,
Guard tales of night beneath the skies.

Each ripple sparkles, soft and bright,
Connecting hearts in soft moonlight.
The trees stand tall, guardians true,
In every breath, nature's debut.

Reflections dance on darkened waves,
Emerald whispers, stories brave.
They cradle sounds of days long gone,
Awakening the universe's song.

A melody of rustling leaves,
And starlit paths that the river weaves.
Together they weave a tale of light,
In moonlit waters, pure and bright.

As night enfolds, the magic calls,
Under the moonlight, wonder sprawls.
Each gleaming wave, each leafy sway,
A symphony of night at play.

A Palette of Ocean and Wood

Brush strokes of blue, the ocean vast,
Where waves and whispers from the past.
A canvas rich with tales untold,
In hues so bright, in colors bold.

The sun dips low, the waters glow,
A fiery dance, a vibrant show.
From sea to shore, the colors blend,
A masterpiece that knows no end.

Seashells gleam with secrets deep,
In tidal pools, where dreams can seep.
With wooden frames, the world stands still,
Captured moments, time's sweet thrill.

Artists walk with gentle grace,
Painting stories of this place.
In shimmering light, reflections play,
A palette where sea and wood convey.

Each brush bristles with whispers sweet,
Creating bonds in every beat.
A world alive with colors true,
An endless ocean, wood, and hue.

Enigma of the Sea's Hidden Glade

In tangled roots, the mysteries lie,
Where shadows dance and secrets sigh.
Fathomless depths with stories spun,
In nature's hold, the riddles run.

Through emerald fronds, the sunlight weaves,
A tangled web of whispered leaves.
The sea's embrace, so warm, so cold,
Harbors tales both new and old.

A hidden glade where shadows play,
Beneath the waves, bright colors stay.
With every breath, the universe speaks,
In gentle waves, and time's own weeks.

Steps through waters, movements slow,
With every ripple, the heartbeats flow.
Secrets linger in salty air,
An enigma wrapped with tender care.

The sea knows well the songs unsung,
In hidden glades, the heart is strung.
From depths to light, the stories throng,
Embraced by the sea, where all belong.

A Symphony of Burgeoning Pines

In the whispering woods, where the tall pines sway,
Their emerald arms cradle the light of the day.
Beneath their embrace, soft secrets entwine,
A symphony plays in the breath of the vine.

With every soft rustle, a tale to be told,
Of dreams spun in shadows, both timid and bold.
The perfume of resin, a chorus divine,
Invites wandering hearts to make their hearts shine.

Sunbeams dance gently on needles of green,
Casting patches of gold on the forest's serene.
Each footstep awakens this haven of peace,
Where worries disperse, and the wild hearts release.

In this tranquil realm, where spirits take flight,
The pines weave their magic, a wondrous delight.
Their majesty echoes, lush stories abound,
In the symphony played, a harmony found.

Into the Depths of Scented Currents

A river of dreams flows with gentle intent,
Its waters enchant, a sweet fragrance sent.
Through petals and blossoms, the whispers abide,
Inviting all seekers to joyfully glide.

The willows lean low, weaving soft tapestries,
With secrets concealed in the rustling leaves' breeze.
Ripples like laughter, a beckoning call,
As treasures await where the mystics enthrall.

Beneath the bright arches of shimmering trees,
Scented currents murmur, embracing the breeze.
With every soft ripple, a story unfolds,
Of lives intertwined, both timid and bold.

Into the depths where the lilies stand guard,
Nature's sweet heart beats, though sometimes it's hard.
In this liquid embrace, all wonders align,
A journey of grace in the space so divine.

Underneath the Glistening Surface

In stillness and silence, the world drifts away,
Underneath water's veil, where the treasures lay.
Pebbles like jewels in a shimmering glance,
Hold stories untold in their luminescent dance.

The lilies, like lanterns, float gentle and bright,
Witnessing secrets in the hush of the night.
Breath of the water, a lullaby's song,
Whispers of peace where the world feels so long.

Beneath, life awakens in ripples and swirls,
A tapestry woven from diamonds and pearls.
Streamlined reflections that catch the soft glow,
Invite tender hearts to dive deep into flow.

With every cool touch of the shimmering tide,
The whispers of nature become our guide.
In the depths, we discover what silence conceals,
A world rich with magic that softly reveals.

Convergence of Nature's Secrets

Where the mountains rise high, and the valleys embrace,
Nature's own canvas, a mystical space.
Here echoes the laughter of rivers on stone,
In each gentle curve, a connectivity sown.

The breeze carries tales of old, wise and profound,
As the clamor of nature sings sweetly around.
Branches entwined in a whispering throng,
Reveal the soft patterns of life's trembling song.

In the key of the forest, notes dance like bright stars,
Uniting the beings, the wild and the scars.
Harmony dwells in each rustle and hum,
In convergence of secrets, our spirits become.

Every flower that blooms holds a wish in its heart,
A connection unbroken sets every part.
As the world spins and twirls in the soft twilight's fold,
We gather the beauty of stories retold.

Perfumed Currents of Coastal Lore

Upon the shore where whispers dwell,
The tide carries tales from sea to shell.
Secrets wrapped in the ocean's embrace,
In the dance of waves, I find my place.

Salted air with a fragrant hue,
Echoes of sailors and dreams anew.
The laughter of gulls, a harmonious song,
Calling to wanderers, where hearts belong.

Seashells scattered, like thoughts unwind,
Each a reminder of treasures we find.
In the twilight glow, the horizon glows bright,
As I weave through the fabric of endless night.

Beneath the stars, ancient voices hum,
Tales of the sea, where we all come from.
Currents that twist like the fables we weave,
In the history of water, we learn to believe.

With every crest, a new story's born,
From the heart of the ocean, forever worn.
Perfumed narratives ride the breeze,
In this coastal world, my spirit finds ease.

The Salty Breath of Ancient Pines

Beneath the boughs where shadows play,
The salty breath whispers of yesterday.
Roots intertwined with tales of the sea,
Guardians of secrets, wild and free.

Tall and proud, they stand in a row,
Witness to storms and the gentle flow.
The scent of the sea, a lover's sigh,
Intertwined with pines, reaching for the sky.

In the rustle of leaves, stories are spun,
Of sailors and mermaids, of moonlit runs.
Branches like arms, they cradle the night,
In their shade, the world feels just right.

As breezes dance through the needle's embrace,
Time moves slowly in this sacred place.
Each whisper of pine holds charm untold,
A tapestry rich, in green and gold.

With every sunrise, a new chapter begins,
Where spirits of nature weave through the winds.
The salty breath, a hymn that calls clear,
In the heart of the pines, I hold what I revere.

Driftwood Dreams and Ocean Spirits

On beaches strewn with driftwood lore,
Each piece tells a tale from the ocean's floor.
Curved and weathered, time's gentle hand,
Crafts dreams of journeys, across the sand.

Waves crash softly, a lullaby's tune,
Summoning spirits beneath the moon.
In twilight's glow, the horizon fades,
And whispers of water, a song cascades.

Beneath the salt, the past intertwines,
Stories of sailors, lost to the brines.
With every driftwood, the tales resound,
Marking the places where wanderers found.

Echoes of laughter, of wild sea days,
Painted in shadows of lingering rays.
The ocean's spirits rise with the tide,
Guiding the heart on a boundless ride.

In dreams of driftwood, I wander far,
Lost in the silence where whispers are.
The ocean's embrace, my solace pure,
In the spirit of water, forever secure.

Fragments of Nature's Assemblage

In the tangle of roots, where moments collide,
Nature's assembly hides treasures inside.
Petals and stones, intertwined with care,
A vibrant mosaic, beyond compare.

Each fragment a story, a memory pinned,
Whispers of seasons that never rescind.
The laughter of blossoms, a gentle refrain,
In the heart of the forest, joy against pain.

Through shadows and light, the colors unite,
A canvas of life, both fragile and bright.
The rustling of leaves, a symphony's call,
In nature's embrace, we rise, we fall.

From the mountains high to the rivers deep,
Fragments of stories in silence we keep.
Each step a reminder, of paths now trod,
In this assemblage, I find my God.

With every breath, a union I feel,
The circle of life, a sacred wheel.
As nature whispers, I find my piece,
In fragments assembled, I discover peace.

The Lilt of Nature's Harmony

In the whispering leaves, the soft winds play,
A melody crafted for the break of day.
Each note a story, each rustle a tune,
Nature's chorus sings beneath the moon.

With every heartbeat, the world sways slow,
Colors collide in an enchanting show.
The streams' gentle laughter, the flowers' sweet sigh,
In this boundless beauty, we learn to fly.

Beneath the vast canopy, shadows engage,
A dance through the hours, turning the page.
Life thrives in harmony, vibrant and bright,
Where daydreams are woven in strands of light.

In soft twilight's hush, the world holds its breath,
For every small moment sings echoes of depth.
The air is alive, infused with delight,
As stars awaken, bidding farewell to light.

Ocean's Breath and Forest's Heart

The ocean whispers secrets only it knows,
Waves like soft hands, in rhythmic repose.
Moonlit reflections dance on the tide,
Where tranquil depths hold treasures inside.

Among the tall pines where shadows reside,
The forest breathes softly, a gentle guide.
Each rustle of branches a tale spun anew,
The wild heart beats in the evening's blue.

Salt and earth mingle, creating a bond,
With every dawn's light, our spirits respond.
There is magic in footsteps upon the soft sand,
And dreams carved in whispers, like castles so grand.

Beneath the vast sky, horizons collide,
In the warm arms of nature, we feel the tide.
A tapestry woven of sea and of limb,
In this life, we flourish, both fragile and grim.

A Tapestry of Aroma and the Deep

In fields of thyme where the sunlight spills,
The essence of earth with each breath instills.
A patchwork of petals, a painter's delight,
Each fragrance a journey, a story in flight.

In gardens of zest, the citrus winds roam,
Awakening senses, they lead us back home.
The spices of life blend into a tune,
A symphony played by the generous moon.

While the ocean's salt air lingers and sways,
The heart of the deep keeps its mysteries at bay.
Shells whisper their histories, soft against sand,
As nature's own canvas sings grand and unplanned.

With hands dipped in soil, we fashion the day,
In the dance of the blossoms, we lose dismay.
A tapestry woven with love and with light,
Where every sweet breath ignites the night.

Tidal Embraces and Verdant Dreams

From the shore's warm embrace, the tides gently pull,
Where whispers of ocean embrace the lull.
Each wave is a heartbeat, a promise, a song,
In the dance of the water, we all belong.

Through emerald canopies, the sunlight weaves,
Our souls intertwine with the rustling leaves.
Each step on the path, a soft heartbeat's call,
In the embrace of the earth, we rise, we fall.

When the stars flicker brightly and dreams start to weave,

Promising futures that none can conceive.
In the forest so lush, or the ocean so vast,
We find hidden treasures in moments amassed.

With the tide rising high, and the day fading low,
A dance in the twilight, where wildflowers grow.
The heart knows its rhythm, a sweet serenade,
In tidal embraces, our fears start to fade.

Whispers of the Deep and Green

In the hush of the emerald glade,
Soft murmurs of secrets invade.
Leaves flutter with tales untold,
As time weaves spells in threads of gold.

Shadows dance in the dappled light,
Nature's breath, a pure delight.
Each whisper lingers, a silent plea,
To bring forth magic from the deep, green sea.

Frogs croak chants of ancient lore,
While crickets sing on twilight's shore.
Underneath the moon's soft gaze,
The forest awakens, begins to blaze.

A silver stream flows with gentle grace,
Reflecting dreams in its embrace.
Rippling waters, a soft caress,
Carry whispers, a soft finesse.

So linger here, in twilight's gleam,
Find solace in the silent dream.
For in the deep and in the green,
The heart of magic can be seen.

Surreal Waters and Fragrant Forests

Where the waters shimmer like glass,
And fragrant blooms begin to amass.
Each ripple paints a story anew,
In hues of lavender and azure blue.

Trees whisper secrets as they sway,
In gentle breezes that come to play.
Dancing shadows flicker and dream,
In this realm where nothing's as it seems.

Fish leap high, catching beams of light,
While blossoms blush in the heart of night.
Surreal wonders weave through the air,
Inviting souls to wander and dare.

The forest's depths hold endless lore,
Of forgotten realms and ancient lore.
With every step on the mossy path,
The echoes linger, their timeless math.

Beneath the stars, the waters hum,
A symphony of nature, sweet and numb.
Let your spirit flow with the streams,
In surreal worlds that cradle dreams.

Secrets Among Pine and Wave

Among the pines where shadows lean,
Secrets whisper, soft and keen.
The ocean's breath a distant call,
Transporting dreams, both small and tall.

Beneath the boughs, where silence sings,
Nature cradles her precious things.
Footsteps muffle on a carpet soft,
As time drifts lazily, like a waft.

Salt and sap intertwine their scents,
Summoning memories, sweet and intense.
Waves break softly, marking the shore,
While pines stand sentinel, evermore.

In the twilight glow, shadows blend,
Gentle sighs that never end.
Hearts entwine in this sacred space,
Finding solace, a warm embrace.

Listen closely, for nature's songs,
Echo peace where the spirit belongs.
Secrets linger, forever entwined,
In the whispers of wave and pine, defined.

Moonlit Paths Through Aromatic Waters

On moonlit paths, where dreams unfold,
Aromatic waters, mysteries told.
Each step a dance on silver beams,
Guided by the light of starlit dreams.

Petals unfurl in the calming night,
Releasing fragrance, a soft delight.
Reflections shimmer, a ghostly glow,
As nature's secrets begin to show.

Breezes carry whispers from afar,
Inviting souls to where wonders are.
The waters ripple with stories spun,
Of moonlit dances, joy, and fun.

Fireflies paint the shadows bright,
With flickering lanterns in the night.
A melody hums, sweet and clear,
Inviting all who wander near.

So roam these paths through fragrant streams,
Embrace the magic, cherish the dreams.
For in moonlit moments, dreams take flight,
In the embrace of aromatic night.

Dreams of Roots and Seafoam

Beneath the waves where shadows play,
Dreams are whispered, night or day.
Roots entwine with tales untold,
In salty depths, the heart is bold.

Stars above in silver gleam,
Guide the wayward in their dream.
The seafoam dances, soft and light,
Crafting stories in the night.

From the pebbled shore to ocean's roar,
Waves carry secrets evermore.
And in the depths where wonders bloom,
Time flows gently, dispelling gloom.

Ancient songs of fear and grace,
Echo through the deep embrace.
Where mermaids weave their luring spells,
And silence holds a thousand bells.

Awake, the mariner hearts so free,
Chasing dreams like fish in the sea.
For every ebb that cradles, holds,
There lies a treasure in the folds.

The Allure of Hidden Galaxies

Beyond the veil where starlight spills,
Lies a universe of whispering hills.
Galaxies twirl in cosmic dance,
Each a riddle, a timeless chance.

Nebulas bloom in colors rare,
Dreams of worlds beyond compare.
Through the void where silence sings,
Hope takes flight on silver wings.

Infinite echoes of wishes made,
In realms where shadows softly fade.
Celestial wonders hover near,
If only we could draw them here.

With every glance at evening's sky,
We seek the stars where secrets lie.
Their allure, a guiding flame,
In a cosmos, we cannot tame.

Yet in our hearts, the spark resides,
A universe where love abides.
For hidden galaxies shall soon unfurl,
The endless beauty of our world.

Songs of the Sea and Growing Trees

Whispers ride the ocean's breath,
Sediments of life and death.
Trees stand tall with roots that cling,
While waves above their praises sing.

In harmony, the sea and land,
Crafting stories hand in hand.
The tides caress the ancient bark,
In twilight's glow, they leave their mark.

Every branch a bell that tolls,
Echoes of forgotten souls.
With every crash, a memory found,
Join the dance, where dreams abound.

Here nature's symphony unfolds,
In rhythms deep and tales retold.
From salty air to fragrant wood,
Immerse in magic, if you could.

So listen close, ye wandering hearts,
For life is woven with its arts.
Beneath the waves and in the trees,
Resides a song that never flees.

Melodies from the Understory

In shadows where the secrets dwell,
Nature weaves its perfect spell.
Murmurs rise from earth's embrace,
Resounding softly, finding space.

Fungi crowned with morning dew,
Sing of worlds both strange and true.
Roots entwined like ancient lore,
Guard the tales they can't ignore.

Crickets chirp a lullaby,
As leaves unfold and spirits fly.
Night's embrace wraps tight and warm,
In the understory, there's no storm.

Life unfurls in whispered tones,
Underneath the canopy's bones.
Each sigh of wind, each tender call,
A symphony that can enthrall.

So wander slow, through these green halls,
Where nature sings and beauty calls.
In every rustle, every breeze,
Life's melodies flow through the trees.

Tranquil Shores and Forest Songs

Upon the shores where whispers blend,
The forest sighs, its branches bend.
Soft sand beneath, a gentle touch,
Time slows down, it means so much.

The waves hum tunes of ages old,
As secrets in the breeze unfold.
The trees sway lightly, nature's dance,
In golden light, we find romance.

With every tide that kisses land,
A tale of wonder, hand in hand.
To breathe the air of peace divine,
In tranquil shores, our hearts align.

Chasing Echoes in Salty Winds

Beneath the sky, a canvas bright,
We chase the echoes, taking flight.
The salty winds, they call our name,
In every gust, a spark, a flame.

The ocean dances, fierce and free,
With whispers of the deep blue sea.
Together, we will wander far,
Under the gaze of every star.

Our laughter mingles with the tide,
In salty air, we find our stride.
Embracing dreams on open shores,
Chasing echoes, forever more.

A Dance of Flavors and Tides

Where flavors twirl on summer's breath,
The sea and land embrace in depth.
A feast adorned with colors bright,
In every bite, a taste of light.

From citrus blooms to herbs so rare,
The tide brings secrets, sweet and fair.
We savor joy in dishes fine,
In melodies of taste, we dine.

As evening falls, the stars appear,
The night unfolds, with joy and cheer.
With every wave and every sound,
A dance of flavors can be found.

Harmonies from Land and Water

In twilight's glow, the earth and sea,
Compose a song in harmony.
With every note that fills the air,
The whispers weave a world so rare.

The rivers' flow, the mountains' song,
In nature's blend, we all belong.
With open hearts, we feel the beat,
As land and water meet and greet.

The cadence sways beneath the moon,
A lullaby, a gentle tune.
In perfect union, life takes flight,
Harmonies that dance through night.